Contents

MALLARD

Common names—Greenhead, Wild Duck.

Adult male in flight—Large size; glossy green head, chestnut breast, silvery-white belly; white wing linings; whitish edges to tail feathers; white bars fore and aft, of purplish-blue wing patch (speculum).

On water—Large size, glossy green head, yellow bill, white collar around neck (incomplete behind). Gray back with longitudinal dark bands; lighter gray sides, reddish orange legs often visible in swimming.

Adult female in flight—Large size, mottled brown duck with white wing linings and whitish tail feathers; two white wing patch bars, as in male.

On water—Large, mottled brown duck with orange bill and legs.

DISTRIBUTION

The whole of the Northern Hemisphere. Domesticated in many parts of the world, especially China, where it is an important source of meat, eggs and feathers.

In North America it breeds regularly from middle states north to Alaska and to the Arctic coast at the mouth of the Mackenzie River. More numerous west of the Mississippi and Hudson Bay.

Winters wherever open water occurs in the interior, sometimes even in Canada; on the Pacific coast from Bering Sea to Mexico; on the Atlantic coast, from the New England states to Mexico. Most abundant in the Mississippi Valley, Gulf coast and northern Mexico. Large numbers winter in Colorado, Utah, Illinois and other central states.

FOOD

Mostly vegetable matter; pondweeds, smartweeds, sedges, bulrush seeds, duck weeds, wild celery, wild rice, sagittaria, acorns; in fact, any good duck food available. On the plains, Mallards feed on the stubble fields of barley, wheat and corn. They take grasshoppers, mosquito larvae and other insects in substantial quantities.

WEIGHT OF ADULTS

Male—Average of 1,577, 2 lbs. 11 ozs. Occasionally birds over 5 lbs. are reported. *Female*—Average of 1,177, 2 lbs. 6 ozs.

Mallard

BLACK DUCK

Common names—Black Mallard, Black, Blackie.

FIELD MARKS

In flight—Sexes alike. Large size, dark head and body, with sharply contrasting *white wing linings*. Upper surface all dusky with purplish wing patch (speculum) barred fore and aft with black. *The trailing edge of the wing patch is margined with white* which is readily seen at close range with the naked eye and at long range with the aid of binoculars. Flight is swift. Keeps well up out of gunshot range. Does not readily decoy. Flies in small flocks on migration—often in "vee" formation or in line. A powerful beat of the wings, which slap the water, lifts it vertically into the air, revealing bright red legs and feet in *adult males,* paler in *adult females.* The bill of the *adult male* is yellow in breeding (winter) plumage, changing to greenish during the post-nuptial (eclipse) moult. *The adult female's* bill is yellowish, dusky-mottled. *Juvenile males* in first winter plumage have greenish, dusky-mottled bills and pinkish-brown legs and feet. *Juvenile females* have greenish, dusky-mottled bills and pinkish feet.

On water—Sexes alike. Large size. General dusky hue, paler on the head and neck. *One white margin to trailing edge* of black-barred, purplish wing patch. Rides buoyantly; swims rapidly.

DISTRIBUTION

Breeding range from North Carolina west to Indiana and Minnesota; north to the northern parts of Manitoba, Ontario, Quebec and Labrador. Casual in Saskatchewan and Alberta. Winters from the Great Lakes to the New England states south to the Gulf coast states.

FOOD

Mostly vegetable matter; pondweeds, grasses, sedges, smartweeds, and grains such as barley, wheat, buckwheat and corn, which they go for in a big way in the fall. Total vegetable matter is about 76 per cent on the coastal marshes, the balance being animal matter—mollusks and crustaceans. Birds in the interior have a larger vegetable diet, about 84 per cent. In the south they turn to rice, acorns, beechnuts and even huckleberries.

WEIGHT OF ADULTS

Male—Average, about 2 lbs. 12 ozs. *Female*—2 lbs. 8 ozs.

Black Duck

GADWALL

Common names—Gray duck, Gadwall.

FIELD MARKS

Adult male in flight—Fairly large size. General gray appearance with a *conspicuous rectangular white patch on hind wing close to body*. The only North American duck with a white speculum (wing patch).

On water: Almost as large as Mallard. Gray duck with velvety black rear end. *White patch (rectangular) high up on side toward tail.*

Adult female in flight—Fairly large size; generally grayish appearance relieved only by the *white patches on wings close to body.* This field mark is unlike that of any other duck.

On water: Grayish duck with small, neat head; yellowish bill and feet. May be easily mistaken for female Mallard or female Pintail. White patch high upon side near tail not always visible and not so prominent as in male.

DISTRIBUTION

The most cosmopolitan of ducks. World-wide in distribution except in South America and Australia. Its breeding range in North America is chiefly on the great plains from the Mississippi west to California; north to southern British Columbia, central Alberta, central Saskatchewan, central Manitoba; east and north to Keewatin (Eskimo Point, Hudson Bay).

Winters from southern British Columbia, central and southern States south to Mexico.

FOOD

The Gadwall seems to dive for food more frequently than other surface feeding ducks, although the young of all species dive quite readily. The Gadwall prefers to feed in the shallow marshes and sloughs where pondweeds, sedges, algae and other aquatic vegetation form more than 90 per cent of its intake. Young Gadwall, during the period of rapid growth, feed largely, if not exclusively, on aquatic and terrestrial insects and larvae.

WEIGHT OF ADULTS

Male—Average of 122, 2 lbs.; extremes, 1 lb. 9 ozs. to 2 lbs. 8 ozs. *Female*—Average of 101, 1 lb. 13 ozs.; extremes, 1 lb. 5 ozs. to 2 lbs. 4 ozs.

Gadwall

BALDPATE

Common names—Baldpate, Baldy, Widgeon.

Adult male in flight—*A conspicuous white, oval-shaped patch on the forewing* is the most distinctive field mark of this species. The lower breast and belly are white. Wing linings white. Utters three or four musically whistled notes which usually are twice repeated in rapid succession.

On water: Rides high, tail well up. Prominent *white forehead and crown* (from which the species gets its name)—creamy-buff in some individuals—is readily seen. Gray neck and brownish body. Tail-end dark with conspicuous white patch between tail and purplish-cinnamon sides. White streak on folded wing.

Adult female in flight—Similar to male but without white cap. *White* wing patches are prominent and distinctive.

On water: Gray head and neck. Brownish body. *White under tail. White streak on folded wing.*

DISTRIBUTION

Baldpates nest more abundantly in western Canada than any other part of their breeding range, which extends from Keewatin (Hudson Bay) west to northwestern Alaska, northern British Columbia, Washington, Oregon and northern California, Nevada, Utah, northern Colorado, Nebraska, Minnesota (probably), Wisconsin and northern Indiana. Rare breeder east of the Mississippi.

Winters from British Columbia south to central America on the Pacific slope and from Massachusetts (rarely) and Chesapeake Bay south to the Lesser Antilles and Costa Rica. In the interior—from the midcontinent States south through Mexico.

FOOD

Baldpates are "hijackers". They often ride herd on Canvasbacks, Redheads and Whitebills (Coots), particularly in fall and winter.

Ninety-three per cent of the Baldpate's food is vegetable matter —pondweeds (Potamogetons), grasses and algae by preference, which it finds in shallow ponds and secures by "tipping-up". It is said to feed much at night. The balance of seven per cent is made up of aquatic insects and mollusks.

WEIGHT OF ADULTS

Males—Average of 12 adults, 1.79 lbs.; of 87 juveniles, 1.70 lbs.
Females—Average of 15 adults, 1.70 lbs.; of 93 juveniles, 1.56 lbs.

Baldpate

AMERICAN PINTAIL

Common names—Sprig; Longneck.

Adult male in flight—Large size; long, streamlined outline; brown head, white underparts and neck—white extends along sides of neck to head. Middle pair of tail feathers greatly elongated and pointed. Speculum (wing patch) shows a prominent white bar on the trailing edge. *On water*—Large, slim, strikingly handsome bird with conspicuous white streak running up side of head. Cannot be mistaken for any other North American duck.

Adult female in flight—Large size, long neck, slim outline. Generally brownish with similar wing patch as male but colors much more subdued. Tail feathers buffy-white. *On water*—Brownish bird, paler on sides of head; long, slim neck; gray bill and feet.

DISTRIBUTION

Most wide-ranging of all North American ducks. Pintails are circumpolar in distribution, the American form having sub-specific status. They breed chiefly west of the Mississippi from the mid-western states to the Rockies and mountain valleys, north to the Arctic coast at Queen Maud gulf, Mackenzie river delta, Alaska and islands of the Bering sea. Recently established (or re-established) as breeders in Nova Scotia, New Brunswick and Labrador. They winter on the Pacific slope from southern British Columbia south to Central America and from Delaware to Florida. The wintering range is practically continuous throughout the southern states, Mexico (excepting Yucatan peninsula) and the Central American republics to Panama.

FOOD

Vegetable matter forms 90 per cent of the adult Pintail's food. Pondweeds, sedges and grasses are most favored but in recent years this species has joined the Mallards in feeding extensively on waste grain on the farm fields. During the first two or three weeks of their lives, young Pintails feed almost exclusively on aquatic and upland insect life. On the land they catch insects with remarkable dexterity.

WEIGHTS

Male—Average of 234 adults, 2.27 lbs.; 390 juveniles, 2.04 lbs.
Female—Average of 63 adults, 1.95 lbs.; 218 juveniles, 1.82 lbs.

American Pintail

GREEN-WINGED TEAL

Common names—Green-wing; Common Teal.

Adult male in flight—Small size, rapid wing beats, speedy flight are features of all teals. At ordinary observing distances, the male shows no distinguishing field marks, which is, in itself, the best identifying feature. Under favorable light conditions the "green flash" of the wing patch (speculum) may be seen. *On water*— Small size. *Narrow, vertical white crescent in front of folded wing,* and *conspicuous yellow-ochre colored spot on the flank* (undertail coverts) are distinctive. This spot varies in color to almost white. At ordinary observing distances field glasses are needed to bring out colors of chestnut head, glossy green patch on sides of head.

Adult female in flight—Small size, rapid wing beats, swift flight and *absolute lack of any distinctive markings* is diagnostic. Brownish (drab) bird with white lower breast and belly. Green flash of speculum may be seen under favorable light conditions. *On water* —Small size; no distinctive markings. Easily confused with females of Blue-winged and Cinnamon teals. The best identification is to see her in company with her mate.

DISTRIBUTION

Breeds in Newfoundland and across the continent from the northern tier of states north to the limit of trees. Nesting range extends southward in the mountainous regions to northern New Mexico. Winters from southern British Columbia and Nova Scotia south through the United States wherever open water can be found, to the West Indies, Mexico and Central American republics.

FOOD

Ninety per cent of the Green-wing's food is vegetable matter but on the Pacific coast many of them feed on rotting salmon, which spoils their flesh for the table. In the interior, where they are restricted to sedges, pondweeds, grasses and other fine duck foods, they are regarded as "tops" for flavor.

WEIGHTS

Male—Average of 130, 12.8 ozs.; extremes, 12 to 14 ozs.
Female—Average of 68, 12 ozs.; extremes, 9 to 13 ozs.

Green=winged Teal

BLUE-WINGED TEAL

Common name—Blue-wing.

Description— A small, swift, surface-feeding duck with pale blue patches on the fore-wing (shoulder), from which the species gets its name. Has increased considerably during last five years.

Male and female in flight—Small size; rapid wing beats; swift. Large pale blue patches on fore-wing—not so prominent in female or juvenile as adult male. These patches appear white under certain light conditions. Small size will separate from Shoveller and Bald-pate with similarly placed wing patches.

Adult male on water—Small size. General appearance dark gray. Vertical white crescent in front of eye. Undertail coverts dark with a prominent white spot on the flank.

Adult female on water—Small size. Lack of any distinguishing marks except when she spreads a wing and reveals the blue patch which otherwise is concealed. Difficult to tell apart from the female Green-winged Teal except by the blue wing patch. Indistinguish-able in the field from the female Cinnamon Teal which also has the blue wing patch. The latter is rare within the breeding range of the Blue-wing, hence chances of confusion are rare. On the water these females are usually found in company with their easily identified mates and that is a convincing identification.

Food

About 70 per cent of the food of the Blue-wing—taken the year around—is vegetable matter, the balance being composed largely of aquatic insects, mollusks and crustaceans. In the interior its feeding habits are such as to impart a delectable flavor to its flesh.

Weights

Average of 73 males—14.6 ounces.
Average of 82 females—13.6 ounces.

Blue-winged Teal

CINNAMON TEAL

Common name—None.

Adult male in flight—Unlike any other duck in North America. Its cinnamon-red general coloration and blue wing patches are as conspicuous as a neon sign. Small size and rapid wing beats are characteristic of all teals. *Adult male on water*—Cinnamon-red of head, neck and body — darker on back — leaves no doubt as to identity.

Adult female in flight and on water—Cannot be distinguished in the field from female Blue-winged Teal. Best identification is to see her in company with her unmistakable mate. The bill is longer and heavier than that of the blue-wing.

DISTRIBUTION

The wintering range is from the southwestern United States south through western Mexico to Panama. The breeding range extends from southern British Columbia into Saskatchewan and Alberta (rarely), Montana, Washington, Oregon, California, Wyoming, Kansas, and states intervening; south to northern Mexico and Lower California.

An entirely separate group of Cinnamon teals occurs in South America from Buenos Aires and the Peruvian Andes to the Falkland Islands and the Straits of Magellan; also from Brazil, Paraguay, Bolivia and Peru (rarely Ecuador and Colombia) to central Patagonia and Chiloe Island. This is the only case of the same species of duck with disconnected ranges in the two hemispheres.

FOOD

Sedges, pondweeds, grasses and smartweeds are preferred foods in the diet, which is 80 per cent vegetable matter. The balance is chiefly insects.

WEIGHTS

Average of 13 males—12 ounces.
Average of 11 females—12.5 ounces.

Cinnamon Teal

SHOVELLER

Common names—Spoonbill; Spoony.

Adult male in flight—Dark head; large bill; white breast; chestnut sides and belly. Chalky-blue patches on fore wings (shoulders) and two diagonal white streaks on back. Whitish tail endings. No other duck like it.

Adult male on water—Bow end down. Heavy bill pointed downwards looks out of proportion with rest of design. Glossy green (or blue) head, very lustrous, which changes color with different angles of view. White breast, chestnut sides, white flank, black rear-end paling to tips of tail feathers.

Adult female in flight—Drab like a mallard female but the outsize, heavy-looking bill is distinctive.

Adult female on water—Like a mallard but bill looks too big for the bird. Lower mandible is reddish-orange. Rides low in front—higher behind.

DISTRIBUTION

Found almost all over the northern hemisphere and in winter in Africa, South America, Hawaii and Australia. One of the most widely distributed of waterfowl. In North America the breeding range is chiefly west of the Great Lakes from Eskimo Point (Hudson Bay), discontinuously through northern Manitoba, the valley of the Saskatchewan River, and up the Mackenzie Valley to its delta and the Alaska coast region south to New Mexico, Arizona and southern California. Formerly through the Mississippi Valley and eastern states where it seems to be making efforts to re-establish itself. Winters from southern British Columbia south on the Pacific side to and including Mexico and Central America, Colombia and the Hawaiian Islands; the southern interior states and the Atlantic Coast from South Carolina and the West Indies.

FOOD

The Shoveller is adept at catching insects. The specialized bill, however, is designed to sift mud and water through the sieve which adorns the edges of the mandibles, and trap the edible material. They seldom tip-up or dive. They also feed on aquatic vegetation but 35 per cent of their food is animal matter.

WEIGHTS

Average of 86 males—1 lb., 3 ozs.; of 68 females—1 lb., 4 ozs.

Shoveller

WOOD DUCK

Common names—Summer duck; Wood duck.

Adult male in flight—Medium size, white breast and belly, white throat and two white bars which extend upward, one toward the eye and the other ending in the black of the hind neck. Chestnut sides of body dark. Dark tail is long for a duck and wedge-shaped —a good field mark. Head is carried above the level of the body, bill pointed down.

Adult male on water—Gorgeous colors, crested head with its conspicuous up-pointed white bars. Black and white crescents in front of wing, and proud carriage, are distinctive.

Adult female in flight—Medium size, swift, direct flight; white breast and belly. Long, wedge-shaped tail. Carries head and bill like male.

Adult female on water—A drab, gray-brown duck with brown elongated crest. A white spot encloses the eye and tapers off to a point behind the eye.

DISTRIBUTION

Breeds from Nova Scotia and New Brunswick west to Manitoba and in southern British Columbia. Summer resident locally in nearly every state in the Union. Winters from southern British Columbia, central Missouri, southern Illinois and southern Virginia south to Jamaica and central Mexico. Rarely north to Michigan and Massachusetts. Casual in Bermuda.

FOOD

Ninety per cent of the food is vegetable matter—duck weeds, cypress cones and galls, sedges and tubers, grasses and grass seeds, pondweeds, acorns and beechnuts, water lily seeds and leaves of water shield; smartweeds, docks, bur-reed, coontail, wild celery, and other available aquatic and terrestrial plants and seeds. Dragon and damsel flies and nymphs, bugs, beetles, grasshoppers, crickets, flies, wasps and spiders make up the bulk of the 10 per cent animal matter consumed.

WEIGHTS

Males—Average of 30, 1 lb., 8 ozs. Females—Average of 13, 1 lb., 2½ ozs.

Wood Duck

REDHEAD

Adult male in flight—Large, puffy-headed duck with heavy looking body, showing black chest in sharp contrast with white breast. The head and neck appear short compared with the Canvasback—the only species with which it is likely to be confused.

Adult male on water—Appears as large as Mallard or Canvasback. Reddish-chestnut head with high brow contour separates it readily from the similarly (less intensely) colored low-brow contoured (wedge shaped) heads of the canvasback. Dark grey back and sides.

Adult female in flight—Large size, head shape and general brownish appearance of head, back and wings with dull-greyish wing patches and white breast, will separate it from the similarly colored females of Canvasback and Lesser Scaup.

Adult female on water—Large size with high brow contour and puffy head. Pale brown color of head serves to distinguish her from female scaup or ring-necked ducks.

DISTRIBUTION

Breeds discontinuously from southern British Columbia, northern Alberta (Athabasca delta), central Saskatchewan (Cumberland House district), central Manitoba (the Pas marshes), south and east to western Pennsylvania (Pymatuning), south-eastern Michigan, southern Wisconsin, northern Iowa, southern Minnesota, central Nevada, and southern California. Winters from southern British Columbia south on the Pacific slope to southern California and the southern tier of states to the gulf coast of Texas south through Mexico; and on the Atlantic coast from Delaware to North Carolina.

FOOD

The Redhead is a diving duck and procures most of its food in that manner. Ninety per cent of its food is aquatic plants, leaves, seeds, roots, and the balance mollusks and insects. Baldpates, Coots and Gadwall often attend the diving Redhead to partake of the fruits of its industry and repay by warning the Redhead of danger.

WEIGHTS

Males—Av. of 70—2 lbs. 8 ozs. Extremes 1 lb. 14 ozs. to 3 lbs.
Females—Av. of 26—2 lbs. 4 ozs. Extremes 1 lb. 6 ozs. to 2 lbs. 11 ozs.

Redhead

RING-NECKED DUCK

Common names—Blackhead, Blackjack, Ringbill, Raft Duck.

Adult male in flight—Black head and chest with white under-parts are similar to the markings of the Scaups and Redhead but the lack of broad white wing patches as in the Scaups and the black head will separate it from those species. Under favorable light conditions a narrow white margin on the trailing edge of the wing, and black head and back, are best field marks.

Adult male on water—Black head and back, grayish-white sides with prominent white crescent between sides and black chest, white ring around bill near tip, are distinguishing field marks. The ring around bill is visible for surprisingly long distances with good binoculars. The chestnut collar around the neck is not visible in the field.

Adult female in flight—Difficult to tell from female Scaups or Redhead. Most reliable clue is to see her with her male.

Adult female on water—White ring around bill is easily seen with aid of binoculars. Whitish face patches are also visible in good light. Both are good field marks.

DISTRIBUTION

Breeds from northwestern Pennsylvania (Pymatuning), Maine, Prince Edward Island, southern New Brunswick, western Nova Scotia, Quebec, southwestern Ontario, northern Michigan, Wisconsin, Minnesota, central Manitoba, northern Saskatchewan, northern Alberta, central Mackenzie valley and south-central British Columbia, south (rarely or formerly) to south-central Oregon, northern Utah, northern Nebraska, northern Iowa and northern Illinois. Winters from southern British Columbia to New Mexico, Arkansas and Texas, and from Massachusetts south in interior fresh-water ponds and reservoirs to West Virginia and Florida, the Bahamas, through Mexico to Guatemala.

FOOD

Vegetable matter forms 80 per cent of the Ring-neck's food. The principal items are water lilies, pondweeds, sedges, grasses, smartweeds, muskgrass and other common aquatics. Insects, mollusks and tadpoles make up the bulk of its animal diet. Although smaller, it is considered by wild game epicures to be equal in flavor to the famed Canvasback and superior to the Bluebill.

Ring=necked Duck

CANVASBACK

Common name—Can.

Adult male in flight—Large size, long head and neck appear dark, black breast, white underbody, dark tail. On migration this species often flies in perfect vee formation, their long, pointed wings carrying them forward with great speed—estimated up to 55 m.p.h.

Adult male on water—Large, white-backed bird with long, wedge-shaped head. The head and neck are reddish-chestnut—clearly seen in good light—darker on crown and throat. Sets low in water and dives almost as quickly and neatly as a loon.

Adult female in flight—Large size and distinctive shape of head are best field marks. Generally darker than male and devoid of contrasting colors. Overall effect brownish, paler on underparts.

Adult female on water—Large brownish bird with yellowish-brown head and neck. The large, wedge-shaped head lacking any brow contour avoids confusion with similarly colored female Redhead.

DISTRIBUTION

Breeds from Alaska (Fort Yukon) and Great Slave Lake to central Manitoba, central western Nebraska, northern New Mexico, northern Utah, and western Nevada, occasionally east to southern Minnesota and southern Wisconsin. Winters from southern British Columbia south along the Pacific coast to Mexico, and from northwestern Montana, northern Colorado, northeastern Arkansas, southern Illinois, and Chesapeake bay south to Florida, the Gulf coast of Louisiana, Texas, central Mexico and rarely, Guatemala. Casual or accidental in Bermuda, New Brunswick and Nova Scotia.

FOOD

Food consists of 80 per cent vegetable matter, the chief items being pondweeds, wild celery, duck potato, grasses (including foxtail and wild rice) ; sedges, water lily, bur-reeds, water milfoil and muskgrass *(Chara)*. The balance—20 per cent animal matter—mollusks, insects, small fish.

WEIGHTS

Male—average of 102, 3 lbs. Extremes 2 lbs., 4 ozs. to 3 lbs., 9 ozs.

Female—average of 102, 2 lbs., 13 ozs. Extremes 1 lb., 14 ozs., to 3 lbs., 6 ozs.

Canvasback

GREATER SCAUP

Common names—Big bluebill, bay broadbill, bay blackhead.

Adult male in flight—A medium-sized black and white duck with a *broad white wing patch* on the trailing edge of wing. This patch is about twice as long as that of the otherwise similarly patterned Lesser Scaup and may be clearly seen when the bird is "going away" as it takes off from the water.

Adult male on water—Indistinguishable from the Lesser Scaup. Black head, neck and chest; bright blue bill, white sides and whitish back; dark rear end—describes both species.

Adult female in flight—Medium size, generally brownish appearance with white breast and belly shading to brown towards tail. White face patch around base of bill. White wing patch as in male but not quite so long. Otherwise indistinguishable from Lesser Scaup.

Adult female on water — Cannot be told apart from Lesser Scaup. The habit of Greater Scaups on migration and on the wintering grounds of rafting in huge flocks in the larger freshwater lakes and saltwater bays, well offshore in the daytime, is a good clue to their identity.

DISTRIBUTION

Breeds in Arctic Europe (also northern Scotland, the Outer Hebrides and Iceland), Arctic Asia and from the Aleutian islands, Alaska and northwestern Canada to the west coast of Hudson bay —more common in the west. Winters south to the Mediterranean, Black and Caspian seas and India (rarely). In America, from the Aleutian islands south to northern Lower California and (occasionally) from Colorado, Nevada, New Mexico and Arizona; also from the Great Lakes and Maine south on the Atlantic coast to North Carolina and on coasts of Florida, Louisiana and Texas.

FOOD

Diet averages 50-50 animal and vegetable matter. Mollusks (including oysters), insects, crustaceans and small fish make up the animal food. Pondweeds, muskgrass, water milfoils, sedges, grasses (including wild rice) and wild celery are the important vegetable foods.

WEIGHTS

Male—Av. of 24, 2 lbs., 1 oz. Extremes 1 lb., 5 ozs. to 2 lbs. 10 ozs.
Female—Average of 18, 2 lbs. Extremes 1 lb., 5 ozs. to 2 lbs. 15 ozs.

Greater Scaup

LESSER SCAUP

Common Names—Bluebill; Broadbill; Fall Duck; Raft Duck; Blackhead.

Adult male in flight—Medium size, short neck, tufty head. Black head, neck and chest; white underbody. Dark wings with broad white wing patch on the secondaries. The Greater Scaup's wing patch extends into the adjoining five or six primaries.

Adult male on water—Medium size; tufty black head; bright blue bill. Shows large amount of white on sides and back—not apparent in flight. Purplish luster on head. Greater Scaup has greenish gloss to head.

Adult female in flight—Medium size; general brownish color; blue bill with white patch on face at base of bill. Whitish underbody and white wing patch. Smaller size of white wing patch is only reliable distinguishing feature compared with Greater Scaup.

Adult female on water—Medium size; brownish head, neck and back. Blue bill with conspicuous white patch around base of bill— a feature also carried by juveniles of both sexes.

DISTRIBUTION

Breeds from the north-central states and southeastern Ontario north through the prairie provinces of Canada and southern British Columbia, to the west coast of Hudson Bay across to eastern Alaska and the Mackenzie Delta.

FOOD

Stomach analysis of 1,051 specimens taken in all months of the year revealed that 59.55 per cent of the food was vegetable matter. Pondweeds, grasses (including wild rice), sedges, wild celery, muskgrass, coontail and smartweeds were preferred foods. The balance of animal matter was made up of mollusks, 25 per cent; insects, 12 per cent; crustaceans, 1.34 per cent, and miscellaneous, 2.13 per cent.

WEIGHTS

Male—Av. of 112, 1 lb. 14 oz. Extremes, 1 lb. 6 oz. to 2 lbs. 5 oz.
Female—Av. of 118, 1 lb. 12 oz. Extremes, 1 lb. 3 oz. to 2 lbs. 2 oz.

Lesser Scaup

AMERICAN GOLDENEYE

Common names—Whistler, Whistle-wing.

Adult male in flight—Medium size; black and white pattern; short neck; big round, black head, and loud, penetrating whistle of wings make identification easy. Shows more white than any other duck except the larger American Merganser. The white wing patch appears to occupy about half the wing area. Round white spot in front of and below eye can be seen under favorable conditions.

Adult male on water—Medium size; large amount of white with black head, back and rear end. Large, tufty head with white spot between bill and eye.

Adult female in flight—Medium size; brownish bird with white breast and whitish wing patch crossed by a dark bar.

Adult female on water—Appears smaller than male and rides lower in water. Brown head and white collar (incomplete behind) are readily seen. *Note:* The female American Goldeneye cannot be distinguished with certainty in the field from the female Barrow's Goldeneye.

DISTRIBUTION

The American Goldeneye is a subspecies of the Goldeneye of Europe and Asia. It breeds from Newfoundland to Alaska wherever suitable nesting sites can be found in the forested regions. It winters from the Aleutians, the southern Canadian provinces and Maine, south, wherever open water is found, to southern California, Arkansas and the states east of the Mississippi to the Gulf coast.

FOOD

About three quarters of the diet is animal matter which probably accounts for its second rating as a table bird. Crustaceans, 32.42 per cent; aquatic insects, 27.98 per cent; mollusks, 9.71 per cent; fishes, 3.16 per cent. Plant food, 26.09 per cent, is chiefly pond-weeds, wild celery, spatterdocks and bulrush.

WEIGHTS

Male—Av. of 36 : 2 lbs. 2½ oz. Extremes, 1 lb. 9 oz. to 2 lbs. 14 oz
Female—Av. of 33 : 1 lb. 11½ oz. Extremes, 1 lb. 6 oz. to 2 lbs. 4 oz.

American Goldeneye

BARROW'S GOLDENEYE

Common name—Whistler.

Adult male in flight—Medium size; black and white pattern; short neck; large, tufty head. Separated from the adult male American Goldeneye by the much larger amount of black on the sides.

Adult male on water—Medium size; large, tufty black head with *purplish sheen and white, crescent-shaped spot in front of eye.* Head feathers, semi-crested, point backwards. Shows more black on back and sides than the American goldeneye.

Adult female in flight—Medium size. Brownish-gray above; white breast. Indistinguishable from female American Goldeneye or from juveniles of both sexes.

Adult female on water—Similar to female American and cannot be separated in life with any degree of certainty.

DISTRIBUTION

Breeds in southern Greenland, Iceland and on the Labrador coast; also from southern Alaska, British Columbia, western Alberta south to California (Sierra Nevada) and southern Colorado. Winters on the Atlantic coast from the Gulf of St. Lawrence to Maine (rarely farther) and on the Pacific coast from southern Alaska to central California.

FOOD

Animal matter constitutes more than 75 per cent of the diet. Salmon eggs and flesh, crustaceans, aquatic insects, larvae and mollusks. Munro's analysis of food taken by specimens collected in the interior of British Columbia revealed 96 per cent animal matter. Vegetable matter is but a small part of its diet and its reputation as a table bird is low.

WEIGHTS

Very little information is available on the weights of Barrow's Goldeneye. Kortright (1942) lists the weights of only one specimen of each sex—Male, 2 lbs., 14 ozs.; Female, 1 lb., 10 ozs.

Barrow's Goldeneye

BUFFLEHEAD

Common names—Butterball, Spirit Duck.

Adult male in flight—Small size. Black and white markings. Large head, short neck, chunky body, rapid wing beats. A broad white patch occupies the mid-section of the wing. A prominent triangular white patch separates the dark feathers of the forehead and hindhead. The dark head feathers are lustrous with purple, green and violet sheens. Lower neck and underparts are white. Back black with a few narrow white feather tips.

Adult male on water—Small size and dominant white appearance contrasting with black back. Relatively large head conspicuously splashed with white makes identification easy. Bill blue-gray; feet flesh-colored.

Adult female in flight—Small size. Generally drab appearance with *small whitish patch below and behind the eye* and white wing patch (speculum) confined to seven inner secondaries. Rapid wing beats; short neck and large head.

Adult female on water—Small size; relatively large head with whitish patch below and behind eye. Otherwise dark brown appearance, darker on back and head. A drab little duck relieved only by the white head spot. Bill bluish-gray; feet dark gray.

DISTRIBUTION

Found only in North America. Breeds from British Columbia, southern Yukon territory, west-central Alaska, northern Mackenzie, Great Slave Lake and southwestern coasts of Hudson and James bays to northern Montana; reported as breeding recently at lakes in northeastern California. Winters from the Aleutians and Commander islands and the Alaska peninsula south to central Mexico and Lower California, and from northwestern Montana, Great Lakes and the coast of Maine to South Carolina, northern Florida and the Gulf coasts of Louisiana and Texas.

FOOD

About 80 per cent of the food is animal matter, insects, crustaceans and mollusks being the chief items. Pondweeds and other aquatic vegetation make up the balance.

WEIGHTS

Male—Average of 17: 1 lb.; extremes, 13 ozs. to 1 lb. 4 ozs.
Female—Average of 14: 12 ozs.; extremes, 8 ozs. to 1 lb. 5 ozs.

Bufflehead

OLD SQUAW

Common names—Long-tailed Duck, Alewife (Scot.).

Adult male in flight—Small size; rapid wing beats. The bird is mostly white with conspicuous black breast and wings. Central tail feathers greatly elongated. Head, neck, upper breast, wings and back are brownish-black. Swift flight with much swerving and turning. Have a habit of towering to great heights and then power diving.

Adult male on water—Head, neck, upper back and most of body are white. Fore part of body is black. Ashy patch around eye, darker spot below and behind eye. Bill is pinkish-orange, with black base and tip. Feet are bluish-gray with darker webs. In summer the head, neck, chest and back are brownish-black.

Adult female in flight—Brown-backed; *white-breasted;* black-winged; white-headed bird in winter plumage. In summer, the head and neck are variegated black and white. The neck and chest are darker, the sides whiter than in winter. In both plumages she lacks the long central tail feathers of the male.

Adult female on water—In winter, stocky, brown-backed; white-breasted and white-headed bird with small bill. In summer, head, neck and chest much darker. Whitish areas of head reduced to patch above and in front of eye and along sides of neck.

DISTRIBUTION

Circumpolar in the Northern Hemisphere. Breeds in Aleutian Islands, Alaska, the Arctic coasts and islands, the tundra, Greenland, Labrador, Iceland, Orkney and Shetland islands, Spitzbergen, northern Norway, Sweden, Finland and Russia; also the Arctic coasts and islands of Siberia. Winters in North America on both coasts and the Great Lakes; as far south as Washington State on the Pacific and North Carolina on the Atlantic.

FOOD

Dives for its food, often to considerable depth, remaining under water for half a minute or more. Almost 90 per cent is animal matter of which crustaceans, mollusks, insects and fishes are the items in order of importance. Grasses and pondweeds are the chief vegetable components. The flesh is tough and fishy.

WEIGHTS

Male—Av. of 21, 1 lb. 13 ozs. Extremes, 1 lb. 9 ozs. to 2 lbs. 5 ozs.
Female—Av. of 10, 1 lb. 10 ozs. Extremes, 1 lb. 2 ozs. to 1 lb. 12 ozs.

Old Squaw

HARLEQUIN DUCK

Common name—Harlequin.

Adult male in flight—Small size; swift flight; rapid wing beats; dark body with reddish sides and curiously placed white spots and streaks leave little room for confusion with any other species.

Adult male on water—Small size; vivid white streaks on neck and breast, and chestnut flanks, conspicuous even in poor light makes identification easy.

Adult female in flight—Small size; dark (drab) appearance, with whitish spots on head and whitish breast; *no white on wings*, will separate from much larger Surf Scoter.

Adult female on water—Small, buoyant, brownish duck with three white spots on head. Care is needed to separate it from the female Bufflehead with one white spot and the female Old Squaw with whiter head and neck.

DISTRIBUTION

Eastern Harlequin breeds in Iceland (resident), Greenland, southern Baffin Island, Labrador and Newfoundland. Casual in Europe and the British Isles. Winters on the Atlantic coast south to Maine—rarely to Long Island, N. Y.

Western Harlequin is found from Baikalia to Anadyr, Kamchatka, Kuriles, Sakhalin; also Pribilof and Aleutian islands, and from Alaska south to the mountains of Montana, Wyoming, Colorado and central California. Winters mainly on the coast, and from the Pribilofs and Aleutians to central California; also on the Asiatic side from the Commander Islands to Japan.

FOOD

About 98 per cent animal matter, made up of crustaceans, 57; mollusks, 25; insects, 10; sea urchins, 2.5; and fishes, 2.5 per cent. The food habits render its flesh unpalatable and it is not hunted to any extent.

WEIGHTS

Male—Average of three: 1 lb. 7 ozs.; extremes, 1 lb. 4 ozs. to 1 lb. 9 ozs. Female—Average of three: 1 lb. 3½ ozs.; extremes, 1 lb. 1 oz. to 1 lb. 5 ozs. Griscom states the female is larger than the male, so it is doubtful if the few records above are representative.

Harlequin

STELLER'S EIDER

Common name—A-noch-a-nee-sak-kuk (Eskimo).

Adult male in flight—Small size; neat, trim outline (as compared with the other heavy-bodied eiders); black and white pattern; white head, dark patch on nape; chestnut-buff breast and belly, shading to paler on flanks. Wings whistle like Goldeneyes in flight.

Adult male on water—Hind part of body and wings black with crescent-shaped white mark on wings; throat, collar and center of back also black. The long scapulars which curve over the white forewing are banded lengthwise with black and white. The bill is grayish-blue and more duck-like than the other eiders. Head white with tufts of greenish feathers behind crown and in front of eye. Eye is encircled by black.

Adult female in flight—Small size; trim outline; dark brown head and body; upper side of wings dark with *purplish-blue wing patch bordered fore and aft with white* like the mallard. Wing linings white.

Adult female on water—Dark brown body with mallard-like speculum.

DISTRIBUTION

Breeds on the Arctic coasts of Siberia and Alaska. Winters on coasts of northern Scandinavia and northern Pacific (Aleutian and Commander Islands, Kuriles and southern Alaska). Accidental in England, Quebec, Greenland, France, Germany, Denmark and Japan.

FOOD

Over 80 per cent animal matter; crustaceans, mollusks, insects, annelid worms, sand dollars, fishes, in that order of preference. Pondweeds, crowberries and algae form the bulk of the small amount of vegetable matter.

WEIGHTS

Male—Average of five: 1 lb. 15 ozs.; extremes, 1 lb. 14 ozs. to 2 lbs. 2 ozs.

Female—Average of five: 1 lb. 15 ozs.; extremes 1 lb. 14 ozs. to 2 lbs.

Steller's Eider

AMERICAN EIDER

Common name—Sea duck.

Adult male in flight—Large size; large, low-hung head, thick neck. Black breast, belly and tail; black and white wings; white back, chest, neck and head. Black crown patch. Flat profile of bill and head gives a wedge-shaped appearance like that of the Canvasback. Fly close to water in heavy, labored flight, although speedy.

Adult male on water—White back, foreparts and black sides.

Adult female in flight — Large size. Uniform dark plumage. Head showing straight-line profile.

Adult female on water—Uniform rich-brown plumage heavily barred with black. Large head and straight-line profile. Swims with bill usually pointed down and neck drawn in.

DISTRIBUTION

The American Eider breeds on coastal islands of Labrador south of Hamilton Inlet, Newfoundland, eastern Quebec, Nova Scotia, and Maine; also on Hudson Bay and James Bay as far north as Southampton Island and Cape Fullerton. Recently, the Hudson Bay Eider has been accorded sub-specific status. The Northern Eider breeds on the coastal islands of Greenland and the eastern Arctic Islands south on the Atlantic coast to Labrador and Quebec. In parts of the winter range they are found in company with the American Eider which winters on the sea coast from Newfoundland and the Gulf of St. Lawrence to Massachusetts and rarely to Virginia. They also interbreed. The Pacific Eider breeds on the Siberian and Arctic coasts, south on both coasts of the Bering Sea and east along the south side of the Alaskan peninsula to Kodiak Island and Cook Inlet. Winters little south of its breeding range.

FOOD

Food consists almost entirely of animal matter (96 per cent); which includes mollusks (chiefly blue mussel), crustaceans, echinoderms (including sea urchins) and insects. A little more plant food is taken during summer.

WEIGHTS

Male—Average of 3: 4 lbs. 6 ozs.; extremes, 3 lbs. 15 ozs. to 4 lbs. 10 ozs. Female—Average of 8: 3 lbs. 6 ozs.; extremes, 2 lbs. 10 ozs. to 3 lbs. 12 ozs.

American Eider

CANADA GOOSE

Common names—Honker—applied to Eastern (Common), Ungava, Great Basin and Western (Pacific) Canada geese.

Adults in flight (Sexes alike)—Large size. Slow, measured wing beats. Dark body; black neck and head with prominent white patch under chin and extending up sides of head to behind eye. Black tail and rump separated by a white bar which is conspicuous when birds take off and are going away.

Adults on water—Large size; grey-brown body; black neck and head and conspicuous white cheek patches.

SUBSPECIES AND DISTRIBUTION

Eastern Canada Goose breeds in the Maritime region of Quebec, Labrador and Newfoundland; winters from Nova Scotia south to Florida. Ungava Canada Goose breeds on the east coast of Hudson and James Bays; in migration to southern United States, mainly west of the Appalachian Mountains. Great Basin Canada Goose from eastern Washington and northeastern North Dakota to northeastern California and central Nebraska. Pacific (Western) Canada Goose ranges from the Queen Charlotte Islands, British Columbia, and along the coast of southeastern Alaska.

These four are the largest forms of Canada Geese. The next two subspecies are smaller. They are the Lesser Canada Goose and the Athabasca Canada Goose. The Lesser breeds from the islands of northeastern Asia east to Baffin Island and winters from northern Washington to northern Mexico. The Athabasca Canada Goose breeds in the northern portions of the Prairie Provinces of Canada and winters as far south as Vera Cruz, Mexico.

The differences are chiefly in body coloration. The Eastern form is a relatively light color; Ungava is darker; Great Basin is the lightest and Pacific the darkest. The Lesser is dark and Athabasca pale.

WEIGHTS

Adult males—Proportion of 1,028 live geese; average, 8 lbs. 4 ozs.; heaviest, 11 lbs. 9 ozs. Juvenile males—average: 7 lbs. 5 ozs. Adult females—7 lbs. Juvenile females—6 lbs. 5 ozs. The Lesser and Athabasca Canada geese weigh between 5 and 6 lbs.

Canada Goose

BLACK BRANT

Common name—Brant.

Adults (sexes alike) on water—Small size (hardly larger than a mallard) short, black head and neck, dark back sharply contrasting with whitish sides. *Tail uptilted showing white undertail coverts.* Rides buoyantly like a gull and is graceful in all its movements.

Adults in flight—The short, black neck and chest contrast sharply with the white breast in the pale-breasted form. The black of the chest shades off gradually into slaty brown of breast and into white of belly in the Black Brant. A white vee over the tail is conspicuous in both forms. The flight is swift, wing beats rapid, wings long and pointed and the birds usually fly in long straggly lines close to water but with frequent changes in elevation. On migration, however, they fly at higher altitudes and sometimes in vee formation.

DISTRIBUTION

The Brant breeds in the Arctic regions from Queen Maud gulf, the Canadian Arctic archipelago, northern Ellesmere and Axel Heiberg Islands, both coasts of Greenland, Spitzbergen and (probably) Fran Josef Land. Winters on the Atlantic coast from New Jersey to North Carolina, less frequently to Massachusetts and Florida and on the Pacific coast of the United States and British Columbia. In Europe to the English Channel, Holland, Germany and Denmark.

The Black Brant breeds on the Arctic coasts and islands from Siberia to Queen Maud gulf in the Canadian Arctic, where it overlaps with the pale-breasted form. Winters mainly on the Pacific coast from Vancouver to Lower California and on the Asiatic side to China and Japan. Accidental on the Atlantic coast and Hawaii.

FOOD

Kortright states, "On their Arctic breeding grounds the food of these birds consists of grass, algae, moss and stalks and leaves of Arctic plants. On the wintering range the preferred food is eel grass *(Zostera)*. Brant are considered the finest table birds of all geese."

WEIGHTS

Males—Average of 21 Black Brant: 3 lbs. 2 ozs.; extremes, 2 lbs. 11 ozs. to 3 lbs. 11 ozs. Female—Average of three Brant: 2 lbs. 6 ozs.; extremes, 2 lbs. 3 ozs. to 2 lbs. 11 ozs.

Brant

EMPEROR GOOSE

Common names—Japanese goose, Not-cha-flick (Eskimo).

Adults on water—Medium size; stocky build; ashy, blue-grey body; white head and hindneck, usually stained with rust; black chin, throat and foreneck. The sharp contrast between black foreneck and white hindneck is distinctive.

Adults in flight—Medium size, chunky outline. All grey body with white head and tail. Flight is swift and usually in line abreast. Rapid wing beats. Orange-yellow feet. Juveniles are similar to adults, except heads are dusky.

DISTRIBUTION

Breeds on the northwest coast of Alaska from the mouth of the Kuskokwim River to the north side of the Seward Peninsula, Point Barrow, St. Lawrence Island, and the coast of Siberia from East Cape to Koliuchin Bay. Winters mainly in the Aleutian Islands and along the Alaskan Peninsula as far east as Bristol Bay, and west to the Commander Islands, straggling to central British Columbia, Washington, Oregon, California and the Hawaiian Islands.

FOOD

The only information on food is the late C. G. Harrold's observations in fall on Nunivak Island, off the northwest coast of Alaska. He states these geese fed mostly along the seashore, but occasional flocks were encountered on the tundra where they were feeding on berries. One adult male specimen had its face stained and the throat and entire intestinal tract dyed blue from a diet of berries.

WEIGHTS

Males—Average of five: 6 lbs. 2 ozs.; extremes, 5 lbs. 8 ozs. to 6 lbs. 12 ozs.

Females—Average of four: 6 lbs. 4 ozs.; extremes, 5 lbs. 2 ozs. to 6 lbs. 14 ozs.

Emperor Goose

WHITE-FRONTED GOOSE
TULE GOOSE

Common names—Specklebelly, Brant, Nuck-luck (Eskimo).

Adults (sexes alike) on water—All dark brown goose except for the *white frontal patch around face at base of bill,* and white upper and lower tail coverts. A whitish line divides the sides and closed wings. (Juveniles lack white face patch in first autumn. This is gradually assumed in winter and spring.)

Adult (sexes alike) in flight—Black- and white-splashed breast. White undertail; orange-yellow legs and feet.

DISTRIBUTION

White-fronted geese breed in the Arctic regions of northeastern Europe, Asia (Siberia eastward) to North America and the west coast of Greenland. In North America, breeds from the Yukon valley east to Anderson river, Clinton Colden lake, Mackenzie and the Perry River district, Queen Maud gulf. Winters in southern Europe and Asia and (in America) from southern British Columbia and southern Illinois south to Louisiana, Texas and Mexico.

Tule geese were found breeding on islands in a fresh-water lake in the Perry river district, Queen Maud gulf in 1941 by Angus Gavin. They kept strictly apart from the smaller White-fronted geese which were also nesting in nearby lakes. They occur in fall migration at the Pas, Manitoba, and Neilburg, Saskatchewan, but no scientific specimens are yet preserved in Canadian institutions. They winter in the Sacramento valley, California.

FOOD

Food consists chiefly of vegetable matter: the tender shoots of grasses, cereal and other grains, berries, beechnuts, and acorns. The small quantity of animal matter comprises aquatic larvae, insects and snails. White-fronts are rated top quality for the table.

WEIGHTS

White-fronts—Males: (average of 21) 5 lbs., 5 ozs. Females: (Average of 17) 4 lbs., 13 ozs. Tule geese—Males: (Average of 16) 6 lbs., 11 ozs. Females: (Average of 12) 5 lbs., 10 ozs.

White-fronted Goose

SNOW GOOSE

Common names—White brant. Wavy, White wavy. Kang-o-wak (Eskimo).

Two forms of Snow geese are recognized—Lesser Snow *(Chen hyperborea hyperborea)* and Greater Snow *(Chen hyperborea atlantica)*. Medium and large-sized geese with all-white plumage and black wing tips.

Adults (sexes alike) on water—Snow-white plumage, large size, pink or reddish bill. Black wing tips partially concealed—*inconspicuous.*

Adult in flight—Snow-white plumage except for *conspicuous* black wing tips. A grey band separates the black primaries from the white part of wing.

DISTRIBUTION

The Lesser Snow breeds in Arctic eastern Siberia and Arctic North America from Point Barrow, Alaska, east to Southampton and Baffin islands and islands northward. Winters in Japan and East Asia; in North America, chiefly west of the Mississippi (especially California), and on the Gulf coast from Florida to Texas and Central Mexico. Casual on the Atlantic coast.

The Greater Snow breeds on northwest Greenland, north Baffin and Ellesmere islands. Winters on the Atlantic coast from Maryland to North Carolina.

FOOD

On the wintering grounds and on migration Lesser Snows feed on roots and culms of aquatic plants and graze like tame geese on fresh sprouts of cereal and ordinary grasses. In autumn they frequent the stubble fields. Berries, wild rice, aquatic insects and small mollusks are part of the diet. Greater Snows feed on sea cabbage, cord grass and sedges which they pull up by the roots. Little is known of their feeding habits on the breeding grounds. Ekblaw describes summering birds as feeding at the bottom of shallow ponds in which *Pleuropogon* (Semaphore Grass) and *Hippuris* (Marestail) were abundant.

WEIGHTS

Lesser Snow—Males: (Average of 19) 5 lbs., 5 ozs. Females: (Average of 18) 4 lbs., 11 ozs. *Greater Snow*—Males: (Average of 19) 7 lbs., 7 ozs. Females: (Average of 12) 6 lbs., 2 ozs.

Snow Goose

BLUE GOOSE

Common names—Blue wavy; Kung-o-vik (Eskimo).

Adults (sexes alike) on water—A dark, medium-sized goose with *white head and neck*. Almost always associated with Lessser Snow geese on land and water, on the breeding grounds, on migration and on the wintering grounds.

Adults in flight—The dusky body and wings contrasting with the white head and neck makes identification easy.

DISTRIBUTION

Breeds on Baffin island in the Bowman Bay region of Foxe Basin, on southwest Southampton island, in the Perry river district, Queen Maud gulf, Arctic Canada, and in the vicinity of Eskimo Point, west coast of Hudson bay. The principal known breeding grounds, discovered by J. Dewey Soper in 1929, are on Baffin island. Winters on the coastal marshes of Louisiana, near the mouth of the Mississippi west—in decreasing numbers—to east Texas.

FOOD

On the Louisiana marshes Blue geese feed on seeds of Sprangletop *(Leptochloa fasicularis)*; Wild millet *(Echinochloa crusgalli)*; the root stocks of Common Three-square Bulrush *(Scirpus americanus)*; the Saltmarsh bulrush *(S. robustus)*; Cord grass *(Spartina patens)* and the Delta Duck Potato *(Sagittaria platyphylla)*. On the tundra, Soper states, "their chief food, for which they grub deep in the soil, appears to be the common tundra grass." During migration on the prairies the birds work over the cultivated fields gleaning waste grain from the previous year's harvest and consuming the tender new shoots of grasses and weeds.

WEIGHTS

Males—(Average of 18) : 5 lbs. 5 ozs.; extremes, 4 lbs. 7 ozs. to 6 lbs. 4 ozs.

Females—(Average of 17) : 4 lbs. 14 ozs.; extremes, 4 lbs. 4 ozs. to 6 lbs. 4 ozs.

Blue Goose

ROSS'S GOOSE

Common names—Little wavy, Galoot, Warty-nosed wavy.

Adults (sexes alike) on water—The smallest of North American geese. All white plumage and black wing tips coupled with small size are best guides to identification. Rides buoyantly on water. The small, neat head and trim appearance give it a "delicate air" which serves to separate it from its larger relative, the Lesser Snow goose, with which it sometimes associates on migration. When seen together the difference in size (the Lesser Snow is twice as large) is conspicuous.

Adults in flight—Ross's goose is much quieter in flight than the garrulous Lesser Snow but, unless they are seen together when the contrast in size can be readily seen, the small size of Ross's is not so appreciable.

DISTRIBUTION

Winters in the San Joaquin and Sacramento valleys of California. Migrates through Montana, Alberta (recorded at Many Island lake, southeastern Alberta; in the Brooks district, south-central; Sullivan lake, east-central; and the Athabasca delta, northern Alberta) ; also at Great Slave lake in the Northwest Territories. Breeds in the Perry river district, Queen Maud gulf, Arctic Canada in approximately 67 degrees 45 minutes north latitude and 102 degrees west longitude. The southward migration follows the same route. Casual in Louisiana, Utah, North Dakota, Manitoba, Saskatchewan, Colorado, Arizona, and Chihuahua.

FOOD

Believed to be chiefly vegetable matter. Grazes on the tender shoots of grass during spring migration. Gavin observed them feeding on Crowberry *(Empetrum nigrum)* on the tundra.

WEIGHTS

Males—Average of 18: 2 lbs. 14 ozs. ; extremes, 2 lbs. 6 ozs. to 3 lbs. 10 ozs.

Females—Average of 19: 2 lbs. 11 ozs. ; extremes, 2 lbs. 5 ozs. to 3 lbs. 7 ozs.

Ross's Goose

KING EIDER

Common Name—King-a-lik (Eskimo).

Adult male in flight—Male distinguished from other eiders by *black back and remarkable shape and coloring of head and bill. The bill is orange with broad shield at base expanding to form a huge and conspicuous knob* in breeding season, rising up to level of top of crown and bordered by black feathers. Crown and nape pale blue-grey; sides of face white tinged pale green; black streak on either side of throat meeting in a vee in front. Upper breast creamy-white, rest of underparts black. Large white patches on forewings and white spot on flank at base of tail.

Adult male on water — Large size. In winter plumage, the creamy-white foreparts, black hindparts and curiously shaped orange bill and frontal shield separated from the blue-grey crown and nape by black, make identification easy.

Adult female in flight—Large size. Uniform rusty or buffy brown. Lighter on throat. Heavily-barred with darker brown. Difficult to identify from other large eider females.

Adult female on water—Large size. Brown, heavily-barred with darker brown. Best identified by association with her consort.

DISTRIBUTION

Circumpolar. Breeds from both coasts of Greenland and entire Arctic coast of Canada and Alaska south to Hudson Strait, northern Labrador, northern Hudson bay, James bay. On the Pacific side, St. Lawrence and St. Matthew islands, and Bering sea. Winters from southern Greenland to the coast of Massachusetts and New York, more rarely to Virginia and the Great Lakes and occasionally farther in the interior, and from Bering sea to the Aleutians, Kodiak and Shumagin islands; also Iceland, Faroes, Great Britain (rare), Norway, Denmark, Holland, north Russia and Finland. Casual in Italy, France, Hungary and south Russia.

FOOD

Almost exclusively animal matter (95 per cent), of which mollusks and crustaceans are predominant. Eelgrass, algae and miscellaneous items make up the small percentage of vegetable matter.

WEIGHTS

Male—Average of 13: 4 lbs.; extremes, 3 lbs. 11 ozs. to 4 lbs. 7 ozs. Female—Average of eight; 3 lbs. 10 ozs.; extremes, 2 lbs. 12 ozs. to 4 lbs. 2 ozs.

King Eider

SPECTACLED EIDER

Common names—Fischer's Eider. Kow-uk (Eskimo).

Adult male in flight—Smaller than Pacific Eider; larger than Steller's. Similar heavy-bodied appearance in flight. Entirely black underparts except throat and neck. White foreback and patches on mid-forewing. Otherwise, wings and lower back and tail are black or dark brown. Head is pale green with *conspicuous white patch around eye which is bordered with black to create the illusion of spectacles*. This feature can be seen at a considerable distance.

Adult male on water—A large sea duck with black sides and tail, white back and throat, yellow bill, pale green head with prominent white patch around eye bordered with black.

Adult female in flight—A dark, almost black duck without conspicuous markings. Indistinguishable from other female eiders except by association with her mate.

Adult female on water—A cinnamon brown eider with heavy black bars on brown feathers. A pale patch around eye—suggesting the spectacles—can be seen at close range.

DISTRIBUTION

Breeds on the Arctic coasts of Siberia and Alaska from the Lena River to Point Barrow (occasionally to Colville River) south, on the Bering Sea coast of Alaska, to the mouth of the Kuskoquim River Winters in the vicinity of the Aleutian and Pribilof islands, and rarely eastward along the south side of the Alaskan peninsula to Sanak island.

FOOD

Little is known of the feeding habits, but studies of the limited numbers of stomachs analyzed disclose that about 75 per cent of the food is animal matter. Mollusks, insects and crustaceans are the most prominent items. Pondweeds, crowberry, marestail and sedges form items in the vegetable diet.

WEIGHTS

Males—Average of 8: 3 lbs. 10 ozs. Extremes: 3 lbs. 3 ozs., to 3 lbs. 12 ozs. Females—Average of 4: 3 lbs. 10 ozs. Extremes: 3 lbs. 6 ozs. to 3 lbs. 14 ozs.

Spectacled Eider

RUDDY DUCK

Common names—Spiketail, Ruddy.

Adult male in flight—Summer plumage: A small reddish-chestnut duck with short, thick neck, black crown, white cheek patches and bright blue bill. White underparts. Readily identified at long distances. Winter plumage: Crown, nape and back dark brown—darker on head. Cheeks and chin, white, underparts white—more or less barred with chestnut or rusty stains. Bill, blue but less brilliant.

Adult male on water — Summer plumage: A perky, reddish-chestnut duck with black brown, conspicuous white cheek patches and bright blue bill. Rides buoyantly in proud, cocky manner with tail often tilted up over the back. Winter plumage: Dark-brown crown and back with white cheeks and blue bill.

Adult female in flight—Chunky, short-necked brownish duck with white underparts, white cheeks divided by a dark stripe and dusky bluish bill. Same in summer and winter.

Adult female on water—Small, dark-brown duck with stiff, longish tail often uptilted. Whitish cheeks appear mottled. Bill, dusky, which looks large in proportion to other features. This latter applies to both male and female.

DISTRIBUTION

Confined to North America. Breeds from central British Columbia, Alberta, and northern Manitoba to western Minnesota, southeastern Wisconsin, southeastern Michigan, northern Illinois, northern Iowa, central Texas, northern New Mexico, central Arizona and northern Lower California; breeding colonies have been found in southern Lower California, the Valley of Mexico and Guatemala. Winters on the Atlantic coast from Chesapeake Bay (more rarely from Massachusetts) to Florida, the Bahamas and West Indies; on the Pacific coast from southern British Columbia to Lower California, Guatemala and Costa Rica and in the interior from central Arizona, southern Illinois and western Pennsylvania southward.

FOOD

About 75 per cent is vegetable matter—pondweeds and bulrush predominating. The balance is insects and other aquatic animal life.

WEIGHTS

Male—Average of 8: 1 lb. 5½ ozs. Female—Average of 8: 1 lb. 2 ozs.